Working Naked

A guide to the bare essentials of home office life

AMERICA'S WORK-FROM-HOME EXPERT

Lisa Kanarek

from the **Working**Naked**.com**® bookshelf

published by Blakely Press

Library of Congress Control Number: 2010911430

ISBN-978-0-615-38303-3

Cover Design by: pounce.com
Copyediting by: Steve Anderson
Book Design by: Laura Wilson, fit to print
                Sarah Miller, shm-art@tx.rr.com

Manufactured in the United States of America

To my sons, Blake and Kyle Weinstein,
who inspire me daily.
I love you both very much.

Contents

The Naked Truth

11. Make the most of home office technology.

12. Give your home office a facelift.

13. Soundproof your home office.

14. Use a few cheap tricks.

SECTION TWO: From chaos to organization

15. Know what belongs on your desk.

16. Store it where you'll use it.

17. Control clutter.

18. Organize your desk drawers.

19. Get by without desk drawers.

20. Use stacking bins over stacking trays.

21. Think vertically.

22. Use a work circle.

23. Find the right office products to meet your needs.

24. Save money when buying office supplies.

25. Store backup supplies in one place.

26. Keep your space organized, especially if clients will visit.

SECTION THREE: Getting paper trained

27. Forget the saying "handle paper once."

28. Sort your papers.

29. Know the difference between three types of files.

30. Follow the P-A-P-E-R system.

31. Set up current files.

32. Put your current filing system into action.

33. Put your files on a diet.

34. Separate current and older files.

35. Purge your files.

36. Follow filing basics.

37. Keep your personal and business papers separate.

38. Color code your files.

39. Solve filing problems.

SECTION FOUR: Getting down to business

40. Know your working style.

41. Discipline yourself.

42. During business hours, keep personal tasks to a minimum.

43. Develop habits that will make you more productive.

44. Control phone interruptions.

45. Plan ahead with children.

46. Plan ahead with pets.

47. Give yourself a break (or two).

48. Balance your home and home office life.

49. Make better use of your time.

50. Stay organized.

The Naked Truth

When I started working naked — working from home without the support of the corporate workplace — almost 20 years ago, my family and friends asked me over and over when I was going to get a "real" office. My home office had everything I needed to run my business, meet my clients' needs and turn a profit, but my choice of comfort and convenience over a commute and corporate environment made it hard for others to take my new home office life seriously.

At first, I didn't let my clients know that I was working

from home. I knew I had to earn their trust and prove that I could do the same job as a business based in a corporate office. Four books, hundreds of articles, many one-on-one consultations and countless seminars later, I'm proud to say that I still work from home. And I'm not alone. With over 34 million home office households in America, the home office stigma is gone. Now it's hard to find someone who doesn't work from home full-time, part-time or after hours.

The 50 tips in this book are ones I've shared with my clients throughout the years to help them gain control over their home offices. These tips have helped them save time so they can focus on both their business and personal lives. If you implement only ten of these tips, don't be surprised to find yourself spending less time fighting meaningless battles with your papers, planning your days and dealing with your physical work space. You'll have more time to spend on productive work and doing what you enjoy.

One of the biggest reasons why working from home

is easier and a more viable option than ever before is ever-changing (and improving) technology. Thanks to high-speed computers, printers/scanners/copiers and of course the Internet, it's possible to do almost any work in a home office that you would expect to be done in a corporate office. This is changing the ways that both corporations and individuals are getting things done.

My specialty is creating functional home offices that fit clients' personal work styles, needs and tastes. Over the years I've noticed that home offices present certain unique challenges. The home office professionals who recognize and deal with these challenges are more effective and more in control.

As you read this book, make sure you have a highlighter in hand and the confidence inside to know that you can change your home office. If you're ashamed of your home office because it's such a mess, take heart: you've come to the right book. No matter how bad you think your office is, I've seen worse.

SECTION ONE:
Bare essentials: Setting up your home office

1. Think location, location, location.

It's important to carefully evaluate every room in your home before you decide the best "real estate" for your office. Even if you've already set up a home office, this is a useful exercise. (There may be a better place for it.) Answering the following questions about each space you might use will help you find the ideal place for your home office:

- Will you actually work in this area?
- Will you be able to keep distractions to a minimum?
- Is there (or could there be) enough lighting?

- How difficult would it be to run phone lines into this space?
- Are there enough electrical outlets?
- Could you set up an Internet connection (in case your home isn't wireless)?
- Is this space comfortable year round?
- Is there room for everything you need (desk, file cabinet, computer, and so on)?
- Is there room for you to display samples of your work (if needed)?
- Is there enough storage space? Or is there room for storage nearby?

Unless you do everything yourself, remodeling is expensive. You may have to spend some money fixing up the right spot for your office. For example, you might want phone lines installed or to have an electrician install effective lighting. Try to think long term. It's better to invest in the right location now than to settle for a space that costs less but won't suit your needs in a year or two. If there's any way to avoid it, you don't want to go through the aggravation of moving your office later.

I've seen people make amazing transformations, turning awkward and inconvenient spaces into organized, efficient, comfortable offices. Consider the following advantages and disadvantages of the various rooms in your home.

THE SPARE ROOM

Advantage: The perfect solution, if you have the space.

Disadvantage: None.

Having an entire room to devote to your office is the ideal situation. You have plenty of space to consolidate everything related to your job, you can work in privacy, distractions are minimized, and you don't have to worry about putting all of your papers away when guests come over. At the end of the day, you can close the door behind you and enjoy the rest of your home. Also, a separate office is the most professional place in which to meet clients.

Before you cross this option off your list, consider whether or not you have a seldom-used room. For example, a dining room could be converted into an office. Attic or loft spaces are other possibilities to consider.

If you have the luxury of converting a spare room into an office, do a thorough job of it. Take the seasonal clothing out of the closet and relocate any hobby equipment you're storing there. Limit everything in the room to work-related items, and use this room only for working. This step is vital to taking a valid home office deduction.

THE GUEST BEDROOM

Advantage: Almost as good as setting up your office in a spare room.

Disadvantage: Inconvenient when guests actually visit.

It's extremely helpful to have your office in a separate, out-of-the-way room that has a door. Rearranging a guest bedroom so that it can accommodate your home office is definitely better than having your office in the corner of a room with more traffic, such as a family room.

If you want your guest room to double as your office (or your office as a guest room), you may have to invest in a hideaway bed, a Murphy bed, or a day bed.

Do you need to keep your guest bedroom relatively intact? You might if you have regular visitors who need access to a bed, a dresser, and some shelves. Use a corner of the room as your office. One of my clients used folding screens to surround her work area. When she stepped behind them and sat at her desk, she was ready to work, and her guests didn't feel they were intruding on her private workspace. Another option is to use a computer armoire.

YOUR BEDROOM

Advantage: It's good to have your office in a separate room, even if it has to be your bedroom.

Disadvantage: Sleeping in proximity to your work.

I usually advise clients not to put their home office in their bedroom unless there's no way to avoid it. However, if you have to choose between setting up

your office in your bedroom or in a portion of another
living area in your home that offers no privacy, choose
the bedroom. The advantages of working in a separate
room without constant interruptions outweigh the
inconveniences of sleeping with your job. With a little
creativity, you can design a workspace that closes up
or is hidden from view after hours. "Out of sight" will
make it easier to sleep with work "out of mind."

When your office is in your bedroom, you'll probably
have limited storage space, so you'll need to think
about other areas where you can store your work-related
materials. And, if clients will be coming to your home,
you'll probably want to clean up the dining room and
meet with them there.

THE LIVING ROOM, DINING ROOM,
OR FAMILY ROOM

> **Advantage:** You have plenty of room to spread
> out your papers while you work.

> **Disadvantage:** In a living area, it's difficult to
> keep your personal life from intruding on your
> work.

When your office is in the corner of a living area of your home, there's constant friction between your work life and your personal life. If you live by yourself, or if you rarely spend time in the area you want to use as a home office, the inconveniences are certainly manageable. (It's faster, for example, to clean up before entertaining). However, if you live with others, they may not be interested in having a home office in their shared living space. You may be interrupted often, your paperwork may be at risk when others have access to your desk, and it will be more difficult to concentrate when you're surrounded by other people's clutter (not to mention your own).

One of my clients successfully turned his living room into a studio. He found it served his needs better than the spare room he had been using. Fortunately, for the most part, he had this territory to himself. During the day, he was alone in the house, and his wife rarely visited the living room unless they were entertaining.

If you live in a one-bedroom apartment and can't

set up your office in your bedroom, you will have
to create a workspace in the living area of your
apartment. You may have to sacrifice the luxury of
having a separate dining area. One helpful tip: Use
high shelves to separate your workspace from the rest
of your apartment.

THE KITCHEN

Advantage: You can stay in contact with your family.

Disadvantage: You are in constant contact with your family.

You may have a kitchen big enough to accommodate
a home office. On the other hand, you may also have
a big family and that could mean your kitchen is the
Grand Central Station of your home. If your kitchen
sees a lot of traffic, expect constant interruptions,
clutter, and distractions when it becomes your office.
If you use the kitchen table as a work area, you'll find
yourself constantly shuffling your papers from place to
place. Despite this, some people prefer working in their
kitchen because they feel comfortable there.

If you set up your office in the kitchen, make sure you have a clear area in which to work and a place to put a two-drawer file cabinet (if you don't have a built-in work area).

THE BASEMENT

Advantage: An out-of-the-way place in which to work.

Disadvantage: Can be depressing: dark, damp, and/or lonely.

A basement office has all of the advantages of an office in a separate room, including privacy, fewer distractions, and a single area in which to put all of your work-related items. If you can transform your basement (or, more likely, a portion of your basement) into a brightly lit, comfortable work area, this is a good option for you. On the other hand, if your basement is damp, musty, or smells awful, working on "the down low" could get old quickly.

THE GARAGE

Advantage: Working in an area separated from the rest of your home that is more private.

Disadvantage: Losing the use of your garage for other purposes.

By remodeling your garage into a home office, you can create a quiet, private workspace that is completely set off from the rest of the house. The downside of creating a garage office is that the remodeling can be expensive. Not only that, but you may miss being able to use that space for parking your car and storing your lawn mower. Depending how big your garage is, you might remodel part of it and share it with your car.

A garage is a good alternative if you want to work at home but still want the feeling of "going to the office" each day. One of my clients, a bookkeeper, liked the freedom of working from home, yet wanted to keep her office and her home separate. She used to have her office in a spare bedroom, but she found she couldn't walk past the door, without going in and doing some work.

Her solution was to convert her garage into an office. She

added insulation and a self-contained heating and cooling unit. When she went to work she would leave through the front door of her house and enter her office through a side door in her garage. By physically separating her office from her home, she was able to feel as though she was working outside her home — without having to commute.

CLOSETS

Advantage: A compact office behind closed doors.

Disadvantages: Limited space, and the loss of the use of your closet for storage.

Sometimes, a large closet can be converted into a nice work area. You'll need to install some overhead shelves for storage, at least one phone line (unless you use your cell phone as your business line), a flat surface for your computer, lighting above and shelves or drawers below, and a file cabinet next to (or under) your work surface. If your closet has sliding doors, you'll need to change them into hinged doors so that both can be open while you work. Another option is to fully open up the length of the closet and install bi-fold doors.

HALLWAYS, ALCOVES, LANDINGS and SPACES UNDER STAIRS

Consider all areas of your home, including wide hallways, alcoves and landings as places for your home office. Again, consider whether these are high-traffic areas or whether they're too secluded to allow you to work.

QUICK TIP: When you're cleaning up, try to decide quickly what to do with each item. Don't procrastinate, because delaying doesn't make the process any easier. Avoid making a "decide later" pile. As you get tired, everything will end up in that pile, and nothing will get thrown out!

2. Make time to clear your space.

1. **Remove any large items** (furniture, skis,
    exercise machines, luggage, and so on) that
    don't belong in your office and store them
    somewhere else. Ask yourself whether you
    really need a television in your home office,
    or whether you're too easily distracted to have
    a TV around.

2. **Use three large boxes to hold any remaining
    smaller items.** The point of using the boxes

is to keep you focused on your office. If you
have to leave to put an item away, you may
get sidetracked. Label the boxes as follows:

- Give away *(charity items)*
- Put away *(items that belong in other
  rooms in your home)*
- Throw away *(items for the trash or
  recycling)*

3. **Work systematically.** Start by decluttering one
   corner of your office area and working your
   way around the room. Progress will be more
   obvious if you focus on just one section at a
   time.

4. **Go back to the large items.** Use the system you
   used for the smaller items: give them away,
   put them somewhere else in your home, or
   throw them out (recycle).

"Decluttering" is a major project, but if you do it right,
you should never have to do it again — or at least not
to this degree. Expect things to look terrible when
your office space is in transition. And don't listen to
comments from your family. You'll only get discouraged.
The end result will be well worth the time you spend.

3. Manage paper overload.

Getting rid of possessions isn't easy. Some folks feel they're throwing away a part of themselves or their history when they "purge." Others hate to get rid of something that's in "perfectly good shape" or that seems as if it may be useful "someday." Clutter interferes with your efficiency because you end up wasting time and energy fixing old items, or searching for the items you need. It's actually far simpler and even cheaper to buy exactly what you need when you need it.

The more you keep, the harder it will become to remember where you've stored things. When I used to do one-on-one consultations, my clients would often remark — as we were clearing out their desks, "I've been looking for that," or, "I didn't even know I had that!" The things you really do need can get buried under the extra items that are only taking up space.

You may be afraid that the minute you throw something away, you'll need it. Everyone goes through that. However, what you have to realize is that before you got rid of those old ice skates, or your books from college, or your baseball trophy from high school, chances are you had either forgotten you had them or forgotten where they were stored. When you keep only those things you need, you'll know what you have and where everything is, and the useful items won't get buried under the items you don't need.

4. Think outside the box.

As you consider your options, keep in mind that you don't necessarily need to set up a traditional office with a big, executive-style desk and an oversized credenza. These days, there are plenty of innovative products on the market — many geared specifically to home office professionals — that allow you to be more flexible in your choices.

If you plan to set up your home office in a living area (such as your living room, dining room, or guest room), consider using a convertible desk or computer cabinet

that's easy to move or that can be closed up when
not in use. When you entertain, all you have to do is
push your office furniture against the wall or close the
"doors" to your office.

There are several good options for convertible desks
and armoires. When searching for one, consider the
following questions.

- Is it big enough to hold your office
  equipment?

- Do you have enough room to work? If you like
  to spread your papers on your desk, you may
  require more space.

Before you buy any type of furniture, make sure each
piece is sturdy, well built and will last. Also, make
sure it will fit through the door, up a staircase or
within a hallway.

5. Furnish your home office your way.

As a home office professional, you should furnish your office however you like. This helps make your office an enjoyable place to work, and if your job involves creativity, it may help you be more innovative.

The downside of furnishing your workspace yourself is that you may have to buy all of your own office equipment, including supplies, furniture, and electronics. This quickly becomes very expensive.

By making good choices, you can get the most out of each expense. Instead of buying a separate printer, scanner and copier, consider an all-in-one model to save space and money. A lateral file cabinet that doubles as a functional work surface could save you the cost of an extra table.

I've found that most people who work from home essentially let their office create itself. Start with basic equipment (such as a computer, and a printer/scanner/copier) and eventually add bookshelves and a higher quality desk chair.

6. Think before you buy furniture.

Before you buy a desk, make sure it's functional, sturdy and ergonomically suited to reduce the risk of straining your back, wrists or elbows. The following are some helpful tips for choosing the major pieces of furniture for your home office.

Desks:

- If you like to tuck things away, buy a desk with only a few drawers or you'll probably end up stuffing things in them.

- If you're not a pack rat, buy a desk that has enough drawer space to hold your everyday items and keep your desktop clear. A desk file drawer is also helpful for keeping papers you are currently working on nearby, but out of sight.

- Buy furniture that holds a monitor, keyboard, CPU and a printer. And think vertically: If there's no place for a CPU, use a holder that stores your CPU on its side under your desk. (An armoire is a great space-saving piece of furniture that allows you to keep all of your equipment in one place.) If you're using a laptop, a smaller writing desk will offer plenty of workspace.

- If you have a limited amount of workspace available, use a printer stand to hold your printer and paper and an undermount keyboard holder (if you don't have a keyboard drawer).

7. Plan out your office furniture arrangement.

- In a home office, you don't need to make your desk face away from a wall or face the door unless clients come to your home.

- If possible, don't put your computer in front of a window. The glare will be hard on your eyes. Make sure your computer screen is either facing a wall without a window or at a right angle to a window, instead of in front of it, for better viewing. If you have to place your computer in front of a window, use drapery or blinds to block the outside light while you're looking at your monitor.

- Don't forget to allow space for opening file cabinet drawers — about an additional 24 inches. The cabinet itself may fit in a convenient space next to your shelves, but it's useless if you can't open the drawers all the way.

- If you have a hideaway bed in your office, make sure you leave enough room in front of it to open and close it easily, especially if you use it often.

8. Find the right chair.

If the office chair you're using now is part of your dining room set, replace it immediately. If you don't, your back will let you know that you've made a big mistake. An office chair should support your back — not interfere with the movement of your arms — and it should absorb and distribute your weight. A few other factors to consider when buying a chair:

- Lumbar support to reduce the strain on your lower back.
- Waterfall seat. The front edge of the seat is rounded to prevent restricted circulation and compression of nerves behind your knees.

- Seat height and back height adjustments.

- Tilt mechanisms and tilt lock to reduce strain and fatigue of your leg muscles.

- Tension control. Reclining tension that should adjust to your body weight for easier reclining.

9. Find functional file cabinets.

Depending on your filing needs and budget, you may want to consider options other than the traditional two- or four-drawer file cabinet. There are a few factors you need to consider:

- How much money do you want to spend?
- How much room do you have in your office?
- How much paperwork do you have?
- What future filing needs do you think you'll have?

File storage options include:

The traditional two- or four-drawer vertical file cabinet.
If you choose one of these, make sure you get a sturdy
cabinet. A bargain, low-quality cabinet may cost you
more in the long run when you have to struggle to open
and close the drawers, replace the handles, or risk
having a drawer fall on your foot. Some file cabinets are
deeper than others, so keep your office space in mind
as you shop.

Lateral file cabinets take up more space horizontally, but
have less depth. One of the nice benefits of a lateral
file is that its top provides a secondary work surface.
You can place the files inside either facing you (front to
back) leaving additional room in the drawers for other
supplies, or the traditional way, side to side.

Open file carts are most often used for work in progress.
However, if you have a limited amount of space in your
office and a limited number of files, a file cart would
work for you. One disadvantage of the open file cart is

that anyone who walks into your home office will be able to see its contents.

File crates with file rods inside will hold a large number of hanging folders. They come in both rigid and collapsible types, with lids and without lids.

Open file crates, similar to milk crates, can be used either on a flat surface, open at the top, or stacked vertically, laid on their sides. If you use a file crate open at the top, you can store hanging folders that hook over the edges of the crate. If you use the crates with the open side facing out, you can use accordion files or file jackets to hold your papers.

Cardboard file boxes with lids are ideal for long-term storage of files that you need to keep but that you know you won't refer to often.

If you have extremely valuable papers you want to file at home, instead of in a safe deposit box, consider investing in a fireproof file box or file cabinet.

If you're a pack rat, don't go overboard with file cabinets. You'll only find a way to fill them up.

10. Measure twice, buy once.

Some people avoid working with a planning grid
because they can't draw. The truth is that you really
don't have to be able to draw to be able to push cutouts
around on a piece of paper. Planning your office on
paper will help you discover some unexpected furniture
arrangements that wouldn't have occurred to you if you
were standing in the middle of your chosen space.

To create a planning grid, use graph paper with half-
inch squares. On the grid, each one-half inch square
corresponds to one foot of office space. You can use

a smaller grid, but probably half-inch squares are
adequate.

Unless you know how to use computer-aided drafting
(CAD), start by penciling a rough aerial (bird's-eye view)
of your office space on a piece of blank paper. Be sure
to include any permanent fixtures, such as windows,
doors, radiators and electrical outlets. (Don't block
any vents if possible.) Then, measure your office space
exactly and draw a more exact layout on grid paper.

After your space is mapped out on the grid, you might
want to run some copies of your layout in case you
want to create a few versions. When you're ready to get
serious, create to-scale cutouts of your office furniture
and move them around on your grid. You'll need
symbols for office items such as the following:

- Desk
- Desk chair
- Credenza
- File cabinet
- Bookcase

- Chairs (for meetings or reading)
- Small conference table

To make the best possible use of your walls, you might consider drawing floor-to-ceiling elevations of your wall space. First, draw anything permanent, such as wall switches or windows. Add any or all of the following:

- Bulletin boards
- Shelves
- Wall clocks

You may find that you want to add some stacking bins to your office, a rolling file cart, or piece of furniture for storage.

11. Make the most of home office technology.

Constantly-evolving technology makes it easy to work from virtually anywhere. The key to making the most of the equipment in your home office is buying the best you can afford.

- **Start with a reliable phone — your link to the outside world.** It affects how you make a first impression. If, while on the phone, you sound as if you are talking into a tin can, you'll make a negative impression. Adding a headset will improve the sound quality, reduce background noise and increase your mobility (if you use a wireless headset). Some home office folks are ditching their land lines altogether and instead are using their cell phone as their business line.

- **Use some type of reliable messaging system, whether voice mail or an answering service.** Check your outgoing message after you record it to make sure you are the only voice and sound on the recording.

- **Take a close look at your computer system to make sure it's still meeting your needs.** Faster is better (A sluggish computer can cost more money in lost business than you would pay to upgrade or replace your system.)

- **Use a printer that's fast and makes high-quality prints.** Keep in mind that if clients aren't visiting your home office, the only image they have of your company may be drawn from the correspondence that you send them. Whatever leaves your home office needs to be top-notch.

The final items to add to your home office are a fax machine or online fax service, a reliable backup system and a copier (depending on how many copies you make a day).

12. Give your home office a facelift.

How would you describe your home office? Does it look a bit rough around the edges? Clients may not see your home office but that doesn't mean it can't be a nice, comfortable and even stylish place to work. Here are a few cheap ways to give your home office a facelift.

- **Paint**. The easiest and cheapest way to update your home office is to paint your walls. Don't be afraid of color. You'd be surprised how anything other than white or beige can change the look and feel of your home office. Finding the right color is easy

if you know where to look. Start with a rug,
a piece of art or any furniture that's in your
home office and then match one of the colors
in it. It doesn't have to be a perfect match.
(That's boring.) If you don't have anything
you want to match, pick a color that inspires
you. If you can't find a color you like, create
your own. I gave up searching for the right
color to match my home office rug and finally
created my own paint color that I proudly call
"Working Naked Gold."

- **Add window treatments**. Add color, pattern and
  interest to your home office by using shades,
  valances or draperies. In the design industry,
  custom = costly. Fortunately, there are some
  great ready-made window treatment options
  available from both high-end stores and
  discount stores.

- **Use homemade accessories**. What better way to
  get art for free than from your kids? Instead of
  tossing out your child's wobbly clay pot, display
  it. My sons' works of art (from a few years ago)
  fill my home office bookcases. They're colorful
  and they have sentimental value.

- **Create cheap (yet stylish) art**. Enlarge your
  favorite photo, add a mat and a frame and
  then hang it. Or buy a book of reproductions,
  clip a few pages, slip them into a frame and
  hang your new masterpieces. Sometimes you
  can find expensive frames on sale.

13. Soundproof your home office.

If your clients think you're calling from a noisy bar instead of your home office, you have a noise reduction issue. Whether your home office could use some serious soundproofing or slight noise reduction, you have a few options.

Soundproofing:

Replace hollow doors with solid doors but leave a small gap at the bottom to let air circulate between rooms.

Replace old — and often ugly — inefficient windows
with double-pane or insulated windows to reduce the
sound from the outside. You'll improve the look of your
home office, decrease your energy bills — and you may
get the added bonus of a tax credit.

Insulate your walls with fiberglass or Sound Attenuation
Batts — lightweight, flexible, fiberglass insulation that
will help absorb and isolate sound waves. (This and the
next tip are easier to do with new construction.)

Add two layers of sheetrock between rooms to reduce
the amount of sound that passes between the rooms. Or
use QuietRock, a soundproof drywall that reduces sound
waves and vibration.

Noise reduction:

Eliminate the cave effect by adding a few throw rugs,
a large area rug or wall-to-wall carpeting to your home
office. This will not only reduce reverberation — but
enhance your positive work vibe by adding color and

another design element to your space.

Add window treatments, including blinds, drapery or even shutters to give sound a place to be absorbed. And hang art on the wall to deflect sound and add a little style and color to your office.

WORKING NAKED

48

14. Use a few cheap tricks.

Creating an efficient home office doesn't have to
cost a fortune. The following tips are for you if you're
interested in saving money:

- Turn an antique buffet, dresser or other piece
  of furniture into office supply storage.

- Instead of buying new bookshelves, add
  shelves in your closet to store samples,
  supplies or books. Create storage space
  in your closet for small office supplies by
  hanging a clear plastic shoe holder.

- Use wire shelves to hold your printer paper or
  letterhead.

- Use a rolling storage system with drawers to store supplies, files or sales materials. You could place a smaller system in your closet to hold backup supplies.

- Place a laminate top, thick sheet of glass or a long board across two file cabinets to create a work surface with storage space below.

SECTION TWO:
From Chaos to Organization

15. Know what belongs on your desk.

An ideal way to decide what should and shouldn't be on top of your desk is to ask yourself the following questions:

- Which items do you use every day?
- Which items do you use at least once a week?
- Which items do you use no more than once a month?
- Are there any items — probably decorative — that you never use?

Anything you use daily (a hand-held or a daily planner, a pen and pencil holder, desk lamp, stapler and tape dispenser) should stay on your desk. Items you use only once a week belong on a secondary surface. Anything you use only once a month should be placed nearby in drawers or on shelves near your desk. Items you seldom use should be stored, and items you never use should be given away or thrown out.

Many people like to personalize their offices with paperweights, photographs, awards, crafts made by their children, and other objects they enjoy. One of the nice things about a home office is that you have the freedom to include in it whatever you like. However, you need to strike a balance between a stark office with nothing but the bare necessities and one so filled with personal items there's no open space in which to work.

Rather than placing knickknacks on top of your desk — your prime work area — move them to another surface. By limiting the items on your desk to those that are work-related and by keeping personal items near — but not on — your desk, you create a more functional work area.

The goal is to leave a space to work and spread out your papers. It's unrealistic to think that everyone can work with a clear desk, but no matter how comforting it may feel to be surrounded by papers, you still need to make room for the papers that need your attention.

If you don't have room for a secondary work surface, add shelves above, below or near your desk.

16. Store it where you'll use it.

Keep related items near one another. For example, store all of your paper — printer paper, letterhead, legal pads (whatever you use) — in the same place.

Keep the items you use often within reach. Items you use occasionally should go in drawers or in a closet in your office. Work-related items or files you rarely use should be boxed up and stored on pallets or shelves in your garage or basement or — if you have the room and cabinet to spare — in a file cabinet. As a last resort, store this rarely used information in another room. But store it together, and limit it to one other room. When you start stashing items around your home, you'll forget what you own. Finally, items you never use should be donated, recycled or placed in your next garage sale. You could even sell them online, but only if you feel the time you spend listing and mailing the items is worth the payoff.

You'll need some files in or next to your desk. These help keep papers off your desk but within easy reach.

Quick Tip: Keep the items you use often within reach. Constantly leaving your desk to get something you need is as big a time waster as searching for lost items. Every time you leave your desk, you waste time and become distracted. It's important to keep in mind that wasted minutes each day turn into wasted hours each week. Those wasted hours will cost money.

17. Control clutter.

To keep your office decluttered in the future, I recommend the following:

- Don't bring anything into your work area without first asking yourself if you really need it.
- Keep only work-related items in your office.
- Whenever an item breaks — whether it's an expensive pen or a printer — get it fixed within a week or get rid of it.

18. Organize your desk drawers.

The fewer junk drawers, the better. They're home
to odds and ends that you "filed" in the drawers to
deal with later. Now is the time to sort through these
items and separate the useful from the useless. The
following steps will take you through this process
quickly:

1. Go through one drawer at a time and take out
   any items you haven't used in the last year.
   These don't belong in your immediate work
   area. Try to make the decision right away
   to throw an item out, give it away, or store

it where you can find it when you need it.
Because space is probably limited, you may
have to be ruthless.

2. Get rid of anything that doesn't work,
   including dead pens or battery-operated
   items that are missing batteries.

3. Get a box for items you can't bear to part
   with. Label this box "Hold." If you still
   haven't used the things in this box after six
   months, get rid of the box.

4. Place all of the remaining items that you use
   often in a pile.

5. Measure a desk drawer that you want to
   use to store small things you use every day,
   such as pens, pencils, tape, scissors, and
   so on. (A lap drawer is best for this.) Then,
   add dividers that fit this drawer to keep your
   supplies from rolling around every time the
   drawer is opened. (There are a multitude of
   office products designed specifically for this
   purpose, but a silverware tray might work just
   as well.)

6. If you have a desk file drawer, use it to hold
   the papers you use often. Keep the papers
   you are currently working on in files instead
   of in piles. You'll need this space for files
   when you start to sort through your papers.

Most desk drawers come with hanging file rods already in them. If your drawer doesn't have a frame in it, you can buy a hanging frame that is easy to assemble, or a freestanding vertical file that fits inside the drawer. You can use either letter or legal-size hanging folders in your drawer, but I recommend letter-size because they take up less room.

7. Now, put the useful items back in your drawers, but this time organized logically. Group like items together, and store the items you use most often within reach. Items you use less often can be less accessible, for example, in the back of a drawer or in a bottom drawer. Items you seldom use shouldn't be in your desk. Store them on shelves elsewhere.

Now that you've organized everything in your desk drawers, you'll never have to waste time searching for lost items. You'll have only one place to look for each item, and you'll be able to see at a glance what you have.

19. Get by without desk drawers.

If you work at a desk or table that doesn't have drawers, you'll need to set up separate holders nearby for the items you use often. If possible, keep these organizers on a secondary surface, not on your desk.

Use any office supply organizer or divided tray to hold your pens, pencils, paper clips, and other small items. Office organizers that fit underneath your printer make efficient use of your work surface.

A desk without file drawers means you'll need a vertical file holder or a file cart (either stationary or on wheels). Not only will you have space for your files, but you'll have extra room to place paperwork you're working on or files you refer to often.

There are many styles, types, and sizes of freestanding vertical file holders. One type is designed to store hanging folders on your desk or on a secondary work surface. The benefits of using this type of vertical file holder (available in plastic, wire, wicker or wood) is that you can use hanging folders for main filing categories and place file folders inside for subcategories.

Another type of vertical file holder holds only file folders. This type has a flat base with equally spaced dividers that stand vertically. Available in wire, plastic or wood, these file holders have a couple of disadvantages: they don't give you the option of using main categories and subcategories when filing your paperwork, and when they get full, it's difficult to see the labels on the folders clearly.

If you'd rather use only file folders, I recommend that you use a tiered vertical file holder. This type of holder makes it easier to see what's being filed where.

Another option for freestanding vertical files is a rolling file cart. A file cart lets you keep files next to your desk when you're working and away in a closet or corner when you're finished for the day or when you have to clean up your office for visitors.

20. Use stacking bins over stacking trays.

There's nothing wrong with stacking trays except that they make it too tempting to shove a piece of paper in a tray and forget about it. (And when you add more trays, it's harder to see what's in the lower trays.) Another option is to use stacking bins. They're larger than stacking trays and can sit on the floor, either under or next to your desk. Stacking bins are inexpensive, easy to use, and small enough to fit any office. They were originally designed to hold vegetables or toys, but they're ideal for organizing papers.

Label each stacking bin. The following are suggested categories for your stacking bins:

- **To Sort.** This bin replaces your In box. When you bring papers into your office (for example, the mail), put them in the To Sort bin until you're ready to process them. You should clear out your To Sort bin by the end of each day or at least every few days.

- **To Read.** This bin is for magazines and newspapers you don't have time to read at the moment but will read later.

- **To Do.** This bin is for papers that need action. Before you put any papers in this bin, you should enter on your to-do list any action you need to take.

- **To File.** Papers that need to be filed in your file cabinet go here. Papers that need to be filed shouldn't be placed on your desk or in your vertical file with papers that need immediate attention.

- **Errands.** This bin is for items you'll need to take with you when you leave your home office. These items could be sales information, letters to mail, or client information to drop off. Using this bin will help you avoid running out to do errands more often than necessary.

Stacking bins are also useful for large projects — for example, a photographer's stack of photographs, a salesperson's new sales materials, or an editor's book manuscripts. When you use them this way, they keep large projects intact and can free up shelf space elsewhere.

Stacking bins provide a temporary place to store papers until you have time to process them. Even if you don't have time to go through them all every day, by using bins you'll know where everything is. After you've read the rest of this book and you have your paperwork and your time organized, you'll get in the habit of going through your stacking bins at least once a week.

21. Think vertically.

A good place to start is with shelves.

- Add shelves above or next to your desk to gain more storage space and to reduce desktop clutter.

- You can use open shelves or a hutch that sits on your desk to increase your storage space.

- Use a tall, four-shelf bookcase — ideally with adjustable shelves — to hold books and reference materials. Adjustable shelves make more sense than fixed shelves because they eliminate wasted space above and below the shelves.

- Attach standards to the wall, insert brackets to hold the shelves, then place the shelves on top. This system is ideal for a closet, but you could also install the system above your desk. This isn't a stylish solution but it's definitely functional.

22. Use a work circle.

Before deciding where to put all of your office items, sit at your desk and imagine a circle around yourself. To make the most productive use of both your office equipment and your time, the items you'll need on a regular basis should be stored in easy reach within that circle.

Are you always reaching into a cabinet or a closet to get pens and pencils? Make them more accessible. Are there books or papers you refer to often? Keep them within arm's reach of your desk. Think of all of the reasons you leave your desk, then try to find a way to eliminate the problem.

23. Find the right office products to meet your needs.

There are mountains of unused office products stashed in closets across the country. Do *not* buy anything that is just going to clutter up your workspace, no matter how appealing it seems.

Some folks keep buying office-organizing products, thinking that each new item will solve their problem of being disorganized. Ironically, these supplies create a new problem: lack of space in which to put all of the new products.

I know many people who are periodically seized by an urge to get organized (usually around the first of the year). They rush to the local office supply store and buy every product guaranteed to save them time, energy, and irritation. Then, mysteriously, their enthusiasm begins to decrease as their frustration with these products increases. Eventually they slip back into their old habits, convinced they'll never be organized and then feel even worse than they did before. Instead of blaming the products, they blame themselves.

Also, I've seen people try to copy their more organized friends by buying the same products and hoping to get the same results. However, the fact that a product works for someone else doesn't mean it will work for you. When it comes to organizing, everyone has different needs, and you have to meet these needs differently.

Instead of trying to adapt yourself to a product — whether it's a vertical file holder, drawer organizer or planning system — find a product that fits your needs. To do this, you need to first identify the areas that are causing you organizational problems.

Once you know what you need, go out and find the right product for you. Then you'll be more likely to use it, and it will be less likely to clutter up your office. Most importantly, you'll be organized.

Quick Tip: Many folks believe that a helpful product should automatically make them organized. Believing that an organizational product should get you organized is like expecting your car to drive you somewhere on its own. Carefully consider any product before you buy it and decide if it will help you get organized or keep you from being organized.

24. Save money when buying office supplies.

Large corporations and small businesses alike waste hundreds, even thousands of dollars each year on unnecessary office supplies. A large corporation may not notice these extra dollars right away, but for small businesses watching every cent, these costs are quickly apparent. Here are a few ways you can keep your office supply costs down.

- **Always use a list when you go to the store**. By using a list, you'll remember to get everything you need and you'll save money by making fewer trips to the store.

- **Buy only what you need, in the quantity you need**. To reduce the amount of time you spend shopping, buy enough office supplies for at least two months. When you first start working in your home office, you won't know exactly how much to buy, but after awhile, you'll develop a pattern and you'll know how long supplies will last.

- **Don't buy more than you can efficiently store**. Buying large quantities of office supplies can be cost effective, but extra supplies won't save you money if they get ruined in the basement, if you forget you have them, or if you can't find them when you need them. If you can't immediately get your hands on a certain item, you'll probably go out and buy another, so you end up replacing what you've already got. Hint: Many supplies are cheaper by the case. Consider splitting the cost with someone else who works from home.

- **Before you buy anything on sale, make sure you need it**. As the saying goes, "If it's on sale, and you don't need it, it's not a bargain."

- **Shop for supplies online** and compare prices before you buy.

- **Buy quality**. Both quality and quantity count. Sometimes when you buy something that

seems like a bargain, you end up getting what
you paid for.

- **Replenish your supplies before you run out.**
  Buying ahead of need gives you a chance
  to comparison shop and take advantage of
  sales. Also, running out at the last minute to
  buy something costs you time and sometimes
  extra money

The type of office supplies you buy or choose not to buy
can make a difference in how effective you are. There
are a few things to keep in mind about office supplies:

- **You can't work without them.** If you've ever run
  out of ink for your printer in the middle of a
  job, you know all too well how one missing
  item can cause your entire workday to grind
  to a halt.

- **Some products are specifically designed to
  keep you organized.** Many office products are
  designed for the sole purpose of helping you
  handle your paperwork and manage your time
  more efficiently, which translates into greater
  productivity.

BASIC HOME OFFICE SUPPLY CHECKLIST

- ❏ Business cards
- ❏ Calculator (unless you use the one on your computer)
- ❏ Check endorsement stamp
- ❏ Clear shoeboxes to hold office supplies
- ❏ Clear tape and dispenser
- ❏ CDs, flash drives or external hard drives
- ❏ Copy and printer paper
- ❏ Daily planner (paper-based or electronic)
- ❏ Drawer dividers (or trays)
- ❏ File folders
- ❏ Hanging file folders (plus clear and colored plastic tabs and inserts)
- ❏ Hanging file frames for file cabinet
- ❏ Highlighter markers
- ❏ Labels or electronic labeler for file folders
- ❏ Scissors
- ❏ Stapler
- ❏ Staple remover
- ❏ Staples

❑ Surge protector(s)

❑ Three-hole punch

❑ Three-ring binders

❑ Vertical file holder

❑ Wastebasket

❑ Manila envelopes (9" x 12" and 10" x 13")

❑ Overnight-delivery packing supplies
    (envelopes and labels)

❑ Paper clips

❑ Pencils

❑ Pens

❑ Printer cartridges

❑ Printer paper

❑ Rubber bands

❑ Stamps

❑ Stationery (imprinted letterhead, plain
    second sheets, imprinted envelopes or high-
    quality paper for letterhead that's printed on
    demand.)

❑ Sticky notes

Add to this list any supplies that are specific to your

business and delete those that don't apply. Then copy

the list and refer to it whenever you're stocking up on office supplies. You could even keep a copy near your supply area (or closet), circling the items you need to buy on your next trip to the store.

Quick Tip: Buy an extra set of office supplies for your family to use (in a color different from the ones in your office). Keep them stored in an area outside your office so that no one will raid your supplies.

Look everywhere for products that might fit your needs. Think out of the (office supply) box:

- A horizontal shoe sorter, with spaces for nine pairs of shoes, is a great place to store forms, sales sheets, or supplies.

- A medium-to-large sized trash can makes the best office wastebasket because you'll spend less time emptying it than you would a small trash can. Hint: Can liners make it easier to empty your office trash quickly.

- A silverware tray makes a perfect drawer divider.

- Use a magazine holder to store envelopes and letterhead vertically.

25. Store backup supplies in one place

When you work from home, it's tempting to store extra supplies in other parts of your home. Instead of looking for additional places to store supplies, cut down on the amount of supplies you already store. Limiting the number of places you have to look for something will limit the amount of time you spend looking. Also, every time you have to leave your office, you run the risk of getting sidetracked in another part of your home.

You can use a closet, an empty dresser, stacking bins, or a

rolling storage system — whatever you like — that works in your office space. What you want to avoid is stashing small piles of extra supplies throughout your office and home.

If you absolutely have to, build shelves for backup supplies in a designated area of your garage or basement. Use this area for items you won't need for a few months. The following ideas will help you store your supplies efficiently so that you'll never hear yourself say, "I didn't know I had that!"

- **Store the same type of supplies together**, so that when you look for something, there's only one place to look. Keep all of your pens, pencils, and markers together and all of your filing supplies together. When all related items are stored together, you're never in doubt about where to find something.

- **Keep supplies — grouped by type — in clear containers**. Label containers and store them next to containers holding related items.

- **Post a list near your supplies to help you keep track of what you have and what you need**. This list should include everything you need to have on hand.

- **Take backup items out of their original packaging to save room.** Those clear containers mentioned already are a more efficient use of space.

26. Keep your space organized, especially if clients will visit.

Having clients come to your home can be stressful and possibly embarrassing. If your home office is organized most of the time and your home office is in a separate part of the house with a separate entrance, you don't have to worry about clients seeing your laundry or your family's mess. If your office is in a living area, however, you need to think about ways to avoid the need for last-minute cleaning sessions before clients show up. You may find it helpful to use a folding screen, or French doors or tall bookcases that set your office apart from the rest of the house, draw attention to your workspace, and hide the rest of your home from view.

In a corporate environment, there are always plenty of desks, but rarely any that are particularly interesting. In a home office, your desk is the center of attention, and it says something about you. Getting it organized and keeping it that way will help you make a professional impression when clients visit your home.

The only room of your home that clients need to see is your office. If possible, have clients use a separate entrance, or locate your office near an entrance. Even though your office may be organized and your presentation professional, you send an entirely different message if you take your clients on a tour through a home that's disorganized.

SECTION THREE:
Getting paper trained.

27. Forget the saying "handle paper once."

When you work in a home office, the only limit on the number of piles of paper you create is the space available in the rooms of your home, and possibly a garage. Throughout my years of helping others sort through mountains of paper, I've figured out that people spread paper throughout their office and home for a few reasons:

- They haven't made a decision about each piece of paper.
- They want to remind themselves of tasks they need to accomplish.

- They're afraid of filing a piece of paper and never seeing it again.

- They don't have specific places to put their papers.

- They want to keep papers around "just in case."

The solution is to follow a simple rule: "Move it forward." Do something to move each piece of paper forward from the minute it comes into your office. You don't have to make final decisions about what action to take, but you do need to decide what you are going to do with the paper involved. First sort, and then file your papers until you need them again.

At first, it will feel strange to do something with each piece of paper instead of just setting it aside. Once you get into this habit, however, you'll no longer have stacks of paper in your office.

28. Sort your papers.

This next task will take time, so make sure you block out at least three hours. The following is a step-by-step plan for sorting all of the papers in your office:

1. **Have on hand, two sturdy boxes and three stacking bins.**

2. **Gather all of the work-related papers** in your office and throughout your home and put the stacks in one area.

3. **Sort these papers into the following five piles**. (Don't stop to read each piece of paper; at this point, you're only sorting.

- **To Do**. These papers need immediate attention. Put them in a stacking bin labeled To Do.

- **To File**. These papers need to be stored in your file cabinet. Put them in your To File stacking bin for the time being.

- **To Read**. This material may include magazines, newspapers, or any other papers you want to read at a later date. These go in your To Read stacking bin.

- **To Sort**. These are papers you need to look at more closely after you've set up a current file system. Put them in one box.

- **To Toss**. Throw out (or recycle) any papers you'll never refer to again, including junk mail. Put these in the second box.

4. **Go back to your To Do bin.** As you look at each piece of paper, enter any action on your To Do list that you need to take. After you've made a note on your To Do list, these papers should be filed in your current file system, which you'll create based on the papers in your To Do bin. Put your To Do papers in the To Do bin until you're ready to set up your Current File system.

If a To Do list won't trigger you to take action, put the papers in the To Do bin and sort through them at the end of the day. This system isn't as efficient as using a To Do list but the point is to keep papers that need action in one place.

The sorting process may seem overwhelming at first, but if you break the project into smaller tasks, you'll have a clearer picture of the types of paper you have — and you'll be able to figure out where your papers should go every day.

One of the biggest benefits of sorting your papers is that you may think twice about saving a piece of paper if you remember that eventually you'll have to deal with it again. Another benefit is that after you finish the sorting process, the next time you have to sort your papers it will take even less time.

29. Know the difference between three types of files.

There are three types of files: *current, reference,* and *historical.* The only similarity among the three is that they all store papers you probably want to see again. Keeping them separate makes it easier for you to get your hands on whatever paper you need when you need it.

- **Current files** contain papers that need your attention. These files could include a letter that needs your response, a report to write, or papers from a project in progress. Current files need to be kept at your fingertips in your desk drawer file, vertical file, file cabinet or in a mobile file cart.

- **Reference files** are those you don't use often, but still need to have accessible. They include any information you may need later on, but not on a daily basis. Examples include papers related to clients, past reports you've completed, letters you've sent, and relevant articles from magazines. Reference files belong in your office in a file cabinet (or similar alternative).

- **Historical files** are files you rarely, if ever, refer to, but need to keep for legal reasons. Examples include past tax returns, inactive client files, paid invoices, or any files over three years old. Historical files should be taken out of your file cabinet and stored away safely in a sturdy box labeled with the contents and date.

Quick Tip: Give your files names that will immediately come to mind when you need a piece of paper. Use word association. There's no general guide to naming files; this is a very individual matter. What works for you may not work for another person. The only filing system that will work for you is one that's customized to meet your needs.

In a home office, you'll probably be the only one using the files, so it doesn't matter if the names mean nothing to anyone else. However, if anyone else will be using your files, explain your system to him or her.

30. Follow the P-A-P-E-R system.

You have five options when it comes to dealing with paper.

Place it in a stacking bin.

Act on it.

Put it in a file.

Enter it on your To Do list and file it.

Rid yourself of it (recycle it).

Place it in a stacking bin (or other temporary holding place).
Stacking bins are a temporary place to put papers you want to read or file. These papers don't require immediate action. Before you put a piece of paper in your To File

bin, write in the upper right-hand corner the name of the reference file where it should go.

Act on it. Acting on a piece of paper means you take action on it at that moment. That could include sending immediate payment to someone or paying a bill right away.

Put it in a file. If you have the time, immediately put papers in the appropriate current or reference files.

Enter it on your list and file it. For papers that need action soon, make a note of what needs to be done on your To Do list on the day you're going to take action. Then, file the paper in the appropriate current file until you're ready to work on it, or temporarily store it in a nearby stacking bin or tray labeled To Do. If you'll need the paper as a backup later but don't need it to work on the project, put it in your reference files. Some current papers may not require a note on your To Do list because they go with information you already have. Put information like this immediately in the correct current file.

Rid yourself of it. This means either recycle it or trash it. The saying "handle paper once" has been used for years. It sounds efficient, but it's not always possible. Instead, do something with each piece of paper to move it forward. For example, let's say you receive a bill from your printer. You handle it the first time when you open it, but it's not bill-paying time yet. So you file the paper in your Bills to Pay file. When you pay the bills, you'll handle it again. There's nothing wrong with handling paper this way. What you want to avoid is picking up a piece of paper, wondering what to do with it, then putting it back in a stack on your desk. When this happens, you haven't done anything to move things forward.

Quick Tip: Avoid piles of paper at all costs! Horizontal piles of paper take up valuable surface space, distract you while you're working, and tend to grow higher and higher as you pile unrelated papers on top of one another. It's easier to find a piece of paper if it is standing vertically in a file with related papers than lying horizontally in a pile with unrelated papers. The time it takes to put papers in file folders is minimal compared to the time it takes to sort through stacks of papers over and over to find the ones you need.

31. Set up current files.

In a desk drawer file, vertical file holder, or rolling file cart, you now want to organize the papers you're currently working on. If you set up a tickler file system, use it with your current files. If you have a hanging file system, use hanging folders. If you're using a vertical file holder that holds only file folders, skip the following steps for hanging folders.

1. **Start by labeling a hanging folder Action**.

2. **Inside this hanging folder, put two file folders labeled To Do and Pending**. (You may want to use Follow-Up instead of Pending.)

3. **Label another hanging folder Bills**. Stagger the plastic tabs on your hanging folders so that you can read them.

4. **Inside this hanging folder, place a file folder labeled Bills to Pay**. If you pay bills twice a month, instead of using Bills to Pay, use two folders labeled 1st and 15th. If you charge any business purchases, add another file folder labeled Charges. Stagger the tabs on the file folders (left, middle, right) so that you can read them. (Consider online bill paying as a way to avoid handling more paper each month.)

5. **Label another hanging folder Projects**. Inside, put a separate file folder for each of your current projects.

6. **Add any other categories you may need, based on the papers in your To Do stack**. For example, you might need a hanging folder labeled Orders, with file folders labeled Orders to Place and Pending Orders.

Avoid labeling any files Miscellaneous. That's an open invitation to keep papers you'll probably never refer to again, or at least won't be able to find.

To be extra organized, use a different color for each group of hanging and file folders. For example, all of your file folders under Bills to Pay could be green.

Quick Tip: Always do what you can to move things ahead. It isn't realistic to think that you can figure out what to do with each piece of paper within minutes. However, you can usually find a way to move things forward if you make an immediate decision and act on it. Even if your decision is to stall, you can file a paper in your current files and make a note on your To Do list to think about it later.

32. Put your current filing system into action.

Before you file anything in your current files, remember to make a note of any action necessary on your To Do list. This will help you get away from keeping papers on your desk to remind you to take care of them. This way your To Do list will take you directly to the right papers. If you want to keep papers out but organized, use a stacking bin labeled To Do. Before you put a piece of paper in that bin, make a note on your To Do list of any action you need to take.

Use the hanging folders and/or file folders you just set up to file your To Do papers. When you come across papers that don't fit into a category you've already created, set them aside until you're finished filing the rest. Then, go back and decide whether you should start a new folder for these papers in your current files, whether they could possibly go in your reference files, or whether you can toss (recycle) them.

- In the To Do folder, put the papers that need immediate action.

- The Pending (or Follow-Up) file folder is for papers that need a response from someone else or some action you need to take at a later date.

- Either file your bills under Bills or "1st" and "15th" depending on how many folders you created for bills. Put charge receipts in a file labeled "Charges." (Later you can compare them against your bill.)

- Group any paperwork about current projects in the Projects hanging folder in the appropriate files. Each project should have its own folder.

Exception 1 is any project that has generated only one or two pieces of paper. Projects with little paperwork can be grouped together in a file folder labeled Ongoing Projects.

Exception 2 is any project that has generated a lot of paper. If a file folder is more than an inch thick, it deserves its own hanging folder, labeled with the name of the project, and filled with separate file folders that correspond to different parts of the project.

After you've sorted your To Do pile, go back to your To Sort pile and decide what to do with those papers. If any of them fall into the To Do category, you now know what to do with them.

When you're finished, there shouldn't be any stacks of paper left on your desk. All of your papers should have been stored in your current files, placed in stacking bins, filed in your reference files or tossed.

33. **Put your files on a diet.**

Current files are for papers that need action. After you're finished with a paper in your current files, it should go in *reference files* or be tossed. Go through your current files often (more than once a year) to get rid of papers that don't belong there. When a file gets too full, look through it for outdated papers that you might be able to toss. It's important to keep papers flowing through your current files. If you don't, your current files will start to fill up with reference files, which will make it harder to find the papers you need right away. It also makes it harder to focus on the tasks that need immediate attention.

A good way to decide which papers to keep and which
ones to eliminate is to take the "Toss or Keep?" test.
It consists of three questions that will help determine
whether or not you should keep something.

1. Have I used this item within the past year?
2. Is it serving a specific purpose?
3. Do I have a place to store it where I can find
   it again?

If you answered "No" to any of these questions,
consider giving or throwing the item away. If you decide
to keep it, make sure you can find it when you need it.

34. Separate current and older files.

Current reference files are different from *current files* because they're used often, but not on a daily basis. Examples of current reference files include the following:

- Backup documents for current projects
- Client files
- Sales materials

Older reference files contain papers from past projects or events. You may look at these files a few times a year. Examples of older reference files include the following:

- Articles from magazines or ones you've downloaded and printed
- Competitive information
- Notes from a seminar you attended
- Past client information

Historical files are files you seldom, if ever, refer to, but need to keep for legal reasons. Examples include past tax returns, inactive client files, paid invoices, or any files over three years old. Historical files should be taken out of your file cabinet and stored away safely in a sturdy box labeled with the contents and date.

As you sort the rest of the papers in your office, think in terms of four file categories.

1. Current
2. Current reference
3. Older reference
4. Historical

Once you get in the habit of thinking this way, all of your filing decisions become much easier.

35. Purge your files.

If you're a pack rat, you may be faced with an overwhelming number of files. Going through your files and keeping only the ones you need may seem to be an impossible task. Don't be surprised if your office looks worse during this sorting process than it did when you started. Keep in mind that this disaster is only temporary, and that when you're finished your office will look much better than it did originally. Still, be prepared for unsolicited advice from family members and friends while you're elbow deep in files.

Throughout the sorting process, don't stop to read every paper. Just sort. It's important to make a quick decision about each file. Here's a step-by-step guide to purging your files:

1. **Sort all your paperwork into four piles**: Current Reference, Older Reference, Historical, and To Sort.

2. **First deal with your historical files**. Put them in sturdy boxes with a lid. Then label them with the date and the contents. Store these boxes in your garage, basement, or attic if you don't have room in your home office. If storage space is limited, you could have them scanned or store them off-site in a storage unit. Before you spend the money on these options, make sure the information you're keeping is worth saving. The point is to keep your historical files out of the mainstream of your home office.

3. **Now turn your attention to your pile of current reference files**. For the next level of organizing, start grouping similar current reference files together. For example, your client files should all be together.

4. **Place your current reference files in the top drawer of your file cabinet,** or the part of the cabinet that is most accessible.

5. **Organize your older reference files into groups,** as you did with your current reference files.

6. **Put your older reference files in the bottom drawer of your file cabinet,** or the part of the cabinet that is least accessible.

7. **Before you go any further, go through each file and take out papers you no longer need.** Avoid the tendency to jump from drawer to drawer. Start with one drawer and work on it until you're finished. As you go through each drawer, you'll find files that belong somewhere else. Either keep them in a stack on the floor until you get to them, or go ahead and place them in the correct drawers.

8. **By now, you should have taken care of all of your historical, current reference, and older reference files, as well as any current files or personal papers that might have sneaked into this process.** Look at your To Sort pile last and decide which category is appropriate for each file. You may be surprised to find, as you look through this pile, that most of the items could be tossed.

36. Follow filing basics.

Before you set up filing systems within your file cabinet,
review the following filing basics:

- Make sure your file cabinet has a frame for
  hanging folders inside. Always use hanging
  folders in your file cabinet, and always
  use file folders inside the hanging folders.
  (Hanging folders are not designed to be taken
  in and out of your cabinet regularly.)

  Some people just stuff their file folders
  in their file cabinet drawer, maybe with
  some cardboard dividers between them.
  This is a bad idea. It will take you longer
  to find the file folder you need because it's

difficult to read the labels on the tabs. With little support, the folders also slip down. Ultimately, you're going to end up ruining folders and making the labels hard to read because you're constantly pushing and pulling on them. When you use hanging folders, you pull on the hanging folder, not on the file folder itself.

- A topic doesn't really deserve its own file folder until you have about eight pieces of paper for it. Another option is to keep information stored electronically.

- Use more than one file folder within each hanging folder. You don't need a separate hanging folder for each project or client until the file folder starts getting too full. Too many hanging folders means too many places to look for one piece of paper. They also take up more space in your file cabinet.

- Keep your folders up to half an inch thick (about 50 sheets). When they get thicker than half an inch, divide the file folder into subcategories. For example, let's say you have a hanging folder labeled Projects, and inside there's a file folder labeled Wilson Project that's getting too big. Divide the Wilson folder into file folders for various aspects of the project. Then, label a hanging folder Wilson Project and put the file folders in it.

- Create an electronic index that lists all of your hanging and file folders. This reduces the chance of creating several files with the same name. Also, when you need to find a piece of paper, the index will help you go to the right file. Keep the index on your desktop for easy access.

- Before you file a piece of paper, always write in the top right-hand corner the name of the file where it belongs. Another option is to highlight a key word that corresponds to a file you've already created. If you need to create a file, write the new file name in the corner of the paper or attach a sticky note with the new file name written on it. You could use preprinted sticky notes that have the word "file" on them.

  When you put the names of the correct files on your papers, the next time you take them out of your file cabinet, you'll know exactly where they belong. You'll also save yourself the headache of creating new files because you weren't sure if a certain file already existed.

- After putting the name of the file in the top

right-hand corner, put a purge date at the top as well. This makes it easier to throw away papers you don't need to keep. Every time you take out a file, throw away any outdated papers. Also, go through your file cabinet at least every six months and get rid of papers you're no longer using.

- Stagger the tabs. Do this on the file folders within each hanging folder and on the hanging folders so that you can easily see each one.

- If you're hard on certain file folders because you're pulling them out a lot, consider buying reinforced file folders that can handle the wear and tear.

•. Avoid filing papers with paper clips attached. These bulk up your files. Even worse, they often catch on other papers and make it difficult to find the papers you need.

37. Keep your personal and business papers separate.

This is especially important if you're taking the home office deduction. If you don't separate business and personal papers, you'll end up constantly looking through your business files to find the personal files you need. Consider keeping personal files in another room, so your spouse won't have to make frequent reconnaissance missions to your office. The ideal approach is to buy a two-drawer file cabinet to use for personal papers. If that's not possible, use one full drawer of your file cabinet for personal papers only.

Quick Tip: If you come across stock certificates, bonds, or the title to your car as you're going through your papers, set them aside until you can put them in your safe deposit box or in a fire-proof safe. Put information about your credit cards — including the card number and the number to call if your card is lost or stolen — in a personal file labeled Important Numbers. Make a copy of the sheet that has the numbers and put it in your safe deposit box or a fireproof safe.

38. Color code your files.

Use color coding to visually separate letters, categories, or numbers. That makes it easy to see what types of files are in your file drawers.

You can use colored hanging folders, colored file folders, and/or colored tabs on the hanging folders, depending on how involved you want to get. Within an alphabetically arranged file drawer, for example, the A's could be red, the B's yellow, and the C's blue. With a categorical filing system, each category could be a different color. With a numerical system, numbers 1 through 25 could be one color, or the files that relate to one another could be one color.

Some home office professionals use different colored folders for different file drawers. Everything in the top drawer, for example, goes in a red folder. This makes re-filing easier. To save money, you could buy colored hanging file tabs only and use file folders inside.

Some folks feel it's easier to get organized when they use colors. If you've had trouble organizing your files, color coding may be the way to go.

39. Solve filing problems.

In my years of helping clients organize their offices, I've discovered a few recurring filing problems. The following are the most common, along with a few solutions:

Problem: File folders are sticking out of the top of hanging folders.

Solution: Limit yourself to four or five file folders within a hanging folder (based on the thickness of each folder). When a hanging folder gets to be 1½ to 2 inches thick, start a new one. Another option is to use a box-bottom hanging folder.

Problem: A file folder is too full.

Solution: Divide the papers into separate file folders, and then put them in one hanging folder labeled with a name that describes the overall category of the file folders.

Problem: Tabs aren't visible on hanging folders.

Solution: Use file folders that are cut lower. Also, make sure your papers are completely in a folder before you put it away.

Problem: You're looking in too many places for a particular piece of paper.

Solution: You're probably using too many hanging folders and too many file folders. Look at your file folders and see which ones could be grouped together in one hanging folder. Don't start a separate file folder until you have five to eight pages of related information. Until that point, group papers with others.

Problem: After taking a file out, you forget where it belongs.

Solution: This is less likely to happen if you keep hanging folders in the file cabinet and take out only the file folder. If you're still having trouble, make sure you keep an updated index of your files. It may also help to color coordinate your file folders so that all folders in one file drawer are the same color.

Problem: You lose papers between hanging folders.

Solution: Make sure you use file folders within hanging folders and always put your papers in a file folder. Some hanging folders are a lighter color inside to help you see that you are placing a file inside rather than outside the hanging folder. You can even buy connectors that join one hanging folder to another, making it impossible to lose papers between hanging folders.

Problem: The file drawer is too full and you can't move the folders back and forth to take file folders out.

Solution: Weed out files and leave about an inch leeway in the file drawer so the folders have room to move.

Problem: You have to shuffle through the folder to find the most current papers.

Solution: Keep the most recent papers in front where they're readily available.

Quick Tip: Some people prefer to file their papers in notebooks or binders instead of file folders. One of my clients, who worked in finance, had, over the years, built up a bookcase filled with binders that were clearly labeled.

If you have more shelf space than file space, try using three-ring binders to free up your file cabinet. This way, you can keep papers such as warranty information on your shelf instead of having them take up space in your file drawers.

Binders will work well if you do the following:

1. Clearly label the outside of each binder.

2. Store related information within one binder.

3. Use dividers within each binder to separate the various sections.

4. Keep a three-hole punch handy to make it easy to quickly punch holes in the papers and put them in binders. If you don't want to punch holes in your papers, use clear plastic sheets that slip easily into a binder.

If you prefer using binders but have more file space than shelf space, there is a way around this problem. Buy binders that hang on file rods.

SECTION FOUR:
Getting down to business.

40. Know your working style.

Everyone works in a different way and has different organizational needs. The techniques I suggest to one client may not work for another. The first step toward knowing which organizational systems will make you more efficient is recognizing your own particular working style.

I've found that most people fall into one of the following five categories:

- **Lookout.** People who like to keep everything in sight. For you, out of sight is out of mind.

You will lay papers out on your desk or even
on the floor to remind you of what needs to
be done. You've probably always functioned
amidst clutter and have never felt it was a
problem. The right organizational systems
for you will enable you to put away your
papers but still keep them at hand and
on your mind. You will find that instead
of keeping an entire project in view, it's
sufficient to keep only a reminder (your to-
do list) in view.

- **Stuffer.** People who like to stuff everything in
  drawers. You are so determined to give your
  home office an organized look that you hide
  things in drawers or closets without taking
  the time to process them first. You've got the
  surfaces under control — which has a calming
  effect on you — but actually, you're generating
  as much clutter as the person who leaves
  everything on top of a desk or on the floor. You
  need organizational systems that will help you
  quickly put things where they belong.

- **Nit Picky.** People who love details and are
  concerned about doing things perfectly,
  no matter how long it takes. You have high
  standards of excellence. You think you're
  organized because the items on your desk
  are perfectly aligned and your file folders are

perfectly labeled. The right organizational systems for you will help you keep your paperwork extremely organized, but with a minimum of obsessing. This will help you focus on the big picture of what you are and are not accomplishing instead of the insignificant details.

- **Bouncing Ball.** People who jump from task to task. You have an active mind and have a hard time focusing on just one thing at a time. You're constantly jumping from project to project without finishing one of them. For example, you make a phone call, then start to write yourself a note about it, but then check your e-mail, which reminds you that you'd like a cup of coffee ... and so on. The right organizational systems for you will help you stay focused on one task at a time so that your productivity increases.

- **Teeter Totter.** Folks who can't make up their minds. You hate making decisions because with every situation you see so many possibilities. It's hard to make decisions because you always have so many options. You're afraid that by committing yourself to one solution, you may be closing off another option that might be better. You need organizational systems that will help you keep moving papers forward, even if you put off making decisions about them.

You may fall into one, two or all of these working styles. You style may depend on the time of day, the type of activity and how difficult the task may be.

41. Discipline yourself.

Effective time management is especially important
when you work from home. Not only are you juggling all
of the roles of accountant, salesperson, manager and
customer service rep, but you're probably finding plenty
of things to do around the house other than professional
work. (Laundry, anyone?) It's interesting and frustrating
how a two-hour project can take 48 hours to complete.
Working your own hours at your own pace is fine, until
the amount of work you produce drops. When you
discipline yourself and get on a regular schedule, you
can be productive and enjoy the benefits of working

from home.

Keep in mind that each interruption and wasted hour means less work accomplished and less income. Some simple changes in the way you run your home office can save you a huge amount of time, which translates into greater success.

It might help to burn the midnight oil. Many home office professionals capitalize on their freedom to work odd hours, particularly at night or on weekends, when there aren't many interruptions. If you don't get as much done during the day as you'd hoped, you can always get in a few hours in the evening. But be careful. For some people, the problem is not knowing when to stop!

42. During business hours, keep personal tasks to a minimum.

When you work in a corporate office, it's understood that you leave your personal life behind as much as possible. When you work at home, however, there is no escaping your personal life, whether it's last night's dishes, phone calls to make, bills to pay, kids to feed, or all of these. To keep from becoming overwhelmed by personal tasks, try the following:

- Set up your home office in a quiet part of the house where you won't be interrupted. If at all possible, claim a spare room.

- Install a separate phone line with voice mail for your business or use your cell phone for business calls.

- Ignore any personal tasks that aren't essential. Otherwise, you could easily spend all day housecleaning instead of working!

- Put off any personal tasks you can accomplish after hours, such as picking up dry cleaning, buying groceries, or making personal calls.

Quick Tip: Design doesn't have to be expensive. Check out eBay, craigslist.com and BradsDeals.com among other sites, for sales on home office furniture and accessories. The Internet makes it easier to find almost anything you need for your home office. If you're willing to take the time to shop online, you'll be amazed at what you can find.

43. Develop habits that will make you more productive.

- **Make your office conducive to working.** Choose an office space you enjoy, and have your office set up so that when you walk in, you can get to work.

- **Set regular office hours.** While you don't have to follow the same rigid schedule you may have had in the corporate world, it's a good idea to set hours for yourself. Otherwise it may be noon before you make your first phone call or answer early morning e-mails. Your schedule can be flexible, but it needs to be one that can help you establish a productive routine.

- **"Go to work" every day**. When you go into
  your office, treat it as you would an office
  away from your home. It definitely takes self-
  discipline to work out of your home, but the
  benefits make the process worth it.

Quick Tip: Don't blame yourself for being
disorganized. Some of my clients are so ashamed
that they ask me to visit their offices covertly
so that no one will know they need help getting
things under control. If you're disorganized, don't
feel guilty. Organizing 101 is a class that few —
if any — schools offer.

44. Control phone interruptions.

Do you ever notice that when you really need to get work done, the phone rings continuously? However, on days when you're not so busy, you may check your phone to make sure it still works? There are a few simple ways to control phone interruptions.

- **Let your voice mail take your calls**. Many folks find it difficult to ignore a ringing phone. When you have a deadline to meet, though, you can't afford to answer every call. Turn your ringer off and use Caller ID to screen calls as you work. You can always pick up the phone if the call is important.

- **Try to avoid playing telephone tag**. When you leave a message for someone, give a specific time when you'll be able to take his or her return call. When you record your own greeting, ask that the caller leave the best time for you to return his or her call and provide your e-mail or Website address in case someone wants to send you an e-mail immediately or needs information right away.

- **Learn how to get off the phone**. When you've finished talking and have the information you need, wind it down. If someone continues talking, ask when you can call back.

- **Take personal calls after hours**. Many people have trouble understanding that home office professionals really work during the day. You may have to let your friends know that you won't be able to take their calls during the day unless there's an emergency. Make plans to call them back after hours at a certain time.

45. Plan ahead with children.

An advantage of working from home is that you get
to be near your children. However, you need to place
limitations on how much time you can spend with them.
When you first start to work at home, your children
may not understand that even though you're home,
you won't be able to spend every minute with them.
Although it's challenging, it's possible to have children
and run a business from home.

- **Expectant parents who plan to work from home
  after their baby arrives may think that babies
  sleep all the time (so they'll have a lot of time**

to work). There's no guarantee that you'll get a baby who sleeps a lot, but even if you do, know that there will still be demands on your time while your child is sleeping.

- **Recognize from the start that if you are serious about your business, you will need some type of childcare.** You can't (and shouldn't) count on television or nap time to keep your child occupied while you work or place business phone calls. If your child has to sleep (or occupy himself or herself) every time you have to work, you will likely add stress to your relationship with your child. There are several child care options to consider, from family day care (your child goes to someone else's house) to at-home child care (a babysitter comes to your home) to a babysitting co-op (you and other parents get together and take turns watching the kids).

- **If you have a preschooler, take him or her to school in the mornings so that you have quiet time to catch up on work.** Don't feel guilty that your child isn't home with you at all times. He or she needs to interact with other children.

- **For the times when your child is with you and you have to take or make a business call, keep**

a box of toys nearby to distract him or her. I recommend, however, that you avoid making business calls with infants and toddlers in the room unless you know your client will understand if they hear a sudden outburst.

- **Set up a little table and chair in your office for your child to use**. Give him or her a smaller version of a telephone, stapler, tape dispenser, ruler, and safety scissors. Add plenty of paper and markers. Your child will be happy to be in the same room with you, and you'll reduce the number of supplies missing from your desk because your child will have supplies of his or her own. To protect your carpet, place a hard plastic chair mat under your child's work area.

46. Plan ahead with pets.

Pets can be a welcome addition to a home office, providing company during the day if you work alone. If you take the time to plan ahead, your pet will be more of an asset than a liability.

- **If you have a dog that barks often, keep it out of your office during work hours — or at least while making phone calls.** It's no fun to be on the phone with a client when your dog spots another dog or squirrel outside.

- **If you have a pet that sheds, take the time to vacuum or sweep your office often.** Otherwise, you run the risk of getting pet hairs in your computer which could damage it or on your visitors which will annoy them.

- **Make sure your pet has plenty of toys to chew on**. I learned this the hard way, after my dog chewed one of my flash drives.

- **Consider getting a second pet to play with the first**. If you're out of your office or need to concentrate on a project, you'll face fewer interruptions because your pets will keep each other occupied.

47. Give yourself a break (or two).

Working by yourself is so demanding that sometimes the thought of taking half an hour for lunch seems impossible. When you work for someone else, there's always somebody around to "hold down the fort," and personal phone calls are often a welcome break throughout the day. None of that applies when you work in a home office.

It's so easy to get involved in what you're doing that you forget to take breaks. Taking breaks throughout the day, however, will actually make you more productive.

It's important to not skip lunch, even if you don't feel ravenous. You're like your car. If you keep driving without stopping for fuel, eventually you're going to run out of gas.

I recommend to my clients who spend hours working at a computer that they stop working periodically throughout the day to give their eyes and brain a rest.

I also recommend walks. A short walk will get the blood pumping and give your brain a breather.

Quick Tip: Don't try to keep your personal and professional lives completely separate. Home office professionals need to find ways to combine their work tasks with their personal tasks in a way that doesn't sacrifice either one. As you plan your day or your week, write down any personal tasks you need to accomplish, but list them separately from your business tasks. This way you can focus on work-related tasks without losing track of personal tasks.

48. Balance your home and home office life.

When you work from home, you're constantly forced to mentally switch from work mode to family mode within minutes. You need to strike a balance between your professional and personal lives, because they happen in the same place. Here are 10 ways to find that balance.

1. **Minimize distractions.** Some people say, "I could never work out of my home because I would have too many distractions." As a rule, minimize trips to the kitchen to get something to eat (except at mealtimes), don't turn on the television, and don't

let yourself get sidetracked by personal activities such as cleaning the house or doing laundry.

2. **Know when to stop working**. A good friend once told me that she could never have a home office because she wouldn't be able to stop working. When you work from home, you don't have far to go when you get the urge to get one more project finished. If you're single, it probably doesn't matter how long you work, but if you have a family, you'll soon hear complaints from all sides. When you stop working, really stop. Close the door to your office or close up your desk and concentrate on your family.

3. **Don't eat lunch at your desk**. When you take a lunch break, leave your office and eat in another part of your home. Changing your scenery and physically removing yourself from your work will help to clear your mind.

4. **Schedule regular "dates" with your spouse and children**. A freelance artist I know blocks out every Wednesday afternoon to spend with her husband. They play golf or tennis or go out to lunch. They both know that every Wednesday afternoon is their time to play, no matter what else is going on during the

rest of the week.

5. **Take at least one weekday off per month to play.** At the beginning of each month, schedule a day when you're going to stay out of your office and do something else. This would be an ideal day to catch up on reading, see a movie you've wanted to see, or just enjoy the outdoors. Let your voice mail take your calls. You'll find that taking a day off will prepare you for a month of productive work.

6. **Make a list of fun things you've always wanted to do, and then start doing them.** Maybe you've always wanted to visit the local art museum. Look online for activities and upcoming attractions. If you've lived in the same city for years, consider taking a guided tour of the city. You'll learn more about your city in a few hours than you have in several years. The point is to keep your horizons open and not let your work consume your life.

7. **Use your office for business-related activities only.** Instead of going to your office to read your favorite magazine or new mystery, go somewhere else in your home. This will keep you in the mindset that your office is for business and the rest of your home is for your personal life.

8. **Don't use other parts of your home for business on a regular basis.** If you have a favorite chair where you sit and read or watch television, don't use it for work. After awhile, you won't feel that it's a place for you to relax and get away.

9. **Include your spouse in your business.** Even though you may work in unrelated fields, it's always good to get an outside point of view. Your spouse may be able to offer you a solution to a problem you've had on your mind for days. Also, if your spouse understands your work and what it involves, he or she will be less likely to resent all of the hours you put into it.

10. **If you and your spouse work together, avoid talking about business after hours.** I know many successful business partners who are also married. They attribute their ability to work and live together to taking the focus off of their work after hours.

Quick Tip: A word about vacations. If you've ever worked for someone else, one week may not have seemed long enough for a vacation. Now that you work for yourself, taking one week off may seem impossible. Do it anyway. At the beginning of each year, block out one-week segments (at least twice) when you'll go on vacation — and treat that time as sacred. Don't schedule appointments during that time, and don't bring work with you if you go away. It's important to recharge your batteries by taking time off.

49. Make better use of your time.

Time management is an overused and misunderstood term. It's not possible to control time; there are only 24 hours in each day and 168 hours in each week. It's possible, however, to control what you do with your time. Making better use of your time will help you overcome the feeling that you're running in place.

Throughout the day, ask yourself if what you're doing is the best use of your time. Every few hours, stop what you're doing and decide whether the task you're working on is the one that needs to be done today or whether it's one that could be done at a later date. You don't have to check up on yourself more often than every three hours; frequent checks would be disruptive. Set the alarm on your watch, on your handheld, or on your computer.

Determine your most productive time of day and schedule important tasks for that time. Some people jump out of bed at 5:00 each morning and are ready to go, while others aren't able to function well until the afternoon. Concentrate on important tasks during the time you're most productive. Leave the less important tasks for when your energy level is low.

Schedule at least one full day a week in the office. If you spend a majority of your time out of the office, set aside one day to spend in your office catching up on paperwork, making phone calls, and planning the following week. Determine which day of the week is slower for you in terms of phone calls you receive or appointments you make, and make that the day you spend in your office. You may have to make an effort to keep that day clear, but if you do, the rest of your week will go more smoothly.

Make appointments with yourself to work on certain tasks. Treat yourself as you would a client, and put yourself on your calendar. Block out certain time periods when you'll work on specific tasks. The task could be a monthly report, a client proposal, or a marketing plan — any activity or project that needs your full attention. Treat this time as an appointment to keep, and make it a productive session. During this time, let your calls go to voice mail and concentrate only on the project you've scheduled. If you wait for an opportune moment to work on projects, it will never come.

Hire outside help if necessary. Virtual assistant businesses continue to grow as demands on our time increase. Small business owners often don't want to hire additional people full time (and they don't need to), so they opt for freelancers. It's easier to hire someone on a project-by-project basis than to bring someone on full time.

There comes a point when you'll realize you can't do everything yourself. Whether the task is entering information into your computer, running errands, cleaning your house, or answering the phone, it's often better to hire someone to do it for you. A good way to decide whether it's worth hiring someone to handle a task is to multiply your hourly rate by the number of hours you estimate the task will take. If your time could be better spent on projects and tasks that would generate income for your business, bring someone in to do the routine tasks that have to be done.

Quick Tip: It's never too late to change. If you want to get organized, you can. If you want to improve, you can. People have different reasons — personal, professional, psychological — for wanting to get organized. Some people realize they're overwhelmed and want to reduce their stress level. Others are ashamed of themselves for being disorganized. Many people would like to have more free time, and everyone would like to have more money. Keep your personal motivation in mind as you implement new organizing skills.

50. Stay organized.

After you've organized your work life, you probably won't go back to your former level of disorganization. The systems you set up after reading this book should fit your needs so exactly that once you get comfortable using them, you'll be happy to maintain them. Still, to keep motivated, it's helpful to do the following:

- Maintain a network of supportive friends and colleagues whom you trust and whose advice you value.

- Talk to others who are where you want to be. You can avoid costly and time-consuming mistakes by talking to those who've already accomplished what you want to accomplish.

- Keep updating your goals and evaluating your progress. Do this on a regular basis — not just when the mood strikes you.

- Keep a positive attitude about yourself and your work.

On the path to working naked:

Don't try to organize everything in one day. It took awhile to get to your current level of disorganization. If you try to do everything at once, there's a high risk of getting discouraged and giving up altogether. Break any project down into manageable chunks and tackle one thing at a time. Make a list of everything you'd like to accomplish, and reward yourself for each task you complete. Scheduling several interruption-free afternoons is usually a more successful approach than trying to organize your entire business life in a day.

There are so many other exciting things to do in life than shuffle paper, react to hourly crises, and increase your stress level.

Don't wait until it's too late. Take the time now to get organized.

Bare Essentials:

The sources listed in this section provide everything from furniture to office supplies.

Home Office Furniture and Supplies:

FURNITURE

aspenhome
www.aspenhome.net
> This line of furniture includes traditional and transitional pieces that fit the décor of most home offices. The pieces are well built and have beautiful finishes.

Ballard Designs

www.ballarddesigns.com

This catalog, popular with interior designers
around the country, offers a wide selection
of desks, rugs, accessories and a majority
of what you need to set up a home office
(minus the electronics). The items they carry
are traditional and transitional and meet the
needs of most home offices.

Caretta Workspace

www.carettaworkspace.com

Solid wood furniture that's stylish, functional
and affordable is rare. The Caretta Workspace
collection offers all of those features and a
bit more. The cable management feature (the
ability to organize tangled power cords) offers
the perfect way to hide your power cords. Not
only do they use solid cherry on their desks,
they offer a locked laptop section that's
temperature-controlled (no more overheating),
monitor holders and built-in lighting.

Computer Furniture Direct

www.cf-direct.com

Home office furniture isn't difficult to find.
Finding furniture to accommodate a monitor,
CPU, printer and other technology must-haves

is a bigger challenge. This site offers solid oak and veneer furniture that has been designed specifically for home office use. Several steps up from Ready-to-Asssemble (RTA) furniture, Computer Furniture Direct offers sturdy pieces that are delivered assembled, which means no need for do-it-yourself skills.

Crate & Barrel

www.crateandbarrel.com

Crate & Barrel has been known more for its household accessories, extensive cooking supplies and decorative place settings, than its home office furniture. But Crate & Barrel has jumped into the home office market with both feet. Its home office line — which ranges from hardwood to pine desks, bookcases and armoires, and traditional to eclectic pieces — is distinctive in that the pieces are designed for longevity. And while their furniture tends to be a bit pricier, you can usually catch a great sale if you're patient.

Desk By Design

www.deskbydesign.com

The furniture on this site projects elegance with its sleek designs and rich materials. If you're looking for an unusual, high-end desk, this is the place to start.

Design Within Reach

www.designwithinreach.com

If you want cutting-edge, non-traditional furniture, this site is worth a look. Touted as a source that "provides easy access to well-designed furniture, frequently found only in designer showrooms," Design Within Reach carries furniture from a long list of designers.

Haworth, Inc.

www.haworth.com

All of their desks and storage units are available through a dealer network. A dealer locator service, complete with detailed maps, is available on their site.

Herman Miller for the Home

www.hmhome.com

Herman Miller, Inc., an international firm that makes and sells commercial and residential furniture, offers a variety of home office furniture, storage and accessories. If you're ready for a new home office but don't know where to start, the Herman Miller "room planner" provides a sleek online tool that will help you to create a custom-made, "virtual" room that's formatted to the dimensions of your home. You can design your office with over

150 pieces of Herman Miller furniture, various windows and doors, and even pets scaled to size (although you'll have to buy or adopt those somewhere else).

Ikea
www.ikea.com
Ikea has a wide selection of cleverly designed furniture available in wood, steel and glass. Some of the units are on strong casters (ideal for a guest room doubling as a home office) and their desk accessories go beyond the typical smoke gray stacking trays and pencil holders. Call or visit their site for a catalog and store locations.

Izzydesign
www.izzydesign.com
Izzydesign features furniture based on a camper's mentality: flexible pieces that are affordable and easy to move. Their clean-looking, versatile designs offer plenty of attractive storage options for a home office of any size.

Knoll

www.knoll.com

> Knoll carries a variety of stylish, yet functional furniture, lighting and accessories for corporate and home office use. Their furniture is designed with ergonomics in mind.

Levenger

www.levenger.com

> Self-described as a provider of "tools for serious readers," Levenger offers a few high-end pieces of home office furniture, plus accessories.

Lizell

www.lizell.com

> High-quality products, including furniture, fill the Lizell catalog. Some of the well-designed pieces are made with cherry veneers and solids and come in various configurations. They offer plush leather chairs and higher-end, ergonomically correct chairs.

Sligh Furniture Company

www.sligh.com

> Check out this great source of contemporary furniture for the home and office.

Steelcase, Inc.

www.steelcase.com

Whether you want freestanding desks, files and storage cabinets or various workstations to house multiple home office staff, Steelcase offers several solutions. Some of their lines use a wood and laminate system of freestanding furniture in traditional and non-traditional shapes and surfaces. While their site doesn't list furniture under "home office," their different lines can be adapted for the at-home worker.

Techline

www.techlineusa.com

Techline manufacturers desk units, computer desks, shelving units and storage. Their Web site can direct you to a Techline Studio or a retailer in your area.

SUPPLIES

Brother International

www.brother-usa.com

Brother's line of labelers are a must-have for easily organizing file folders, containers and supplies. Brother also offers a full line of All-in-One machines (printers, faxes, scanners, copiers).

The Container Store
www.containerstore.com

As the name implies, you'll find virtually every organizing product on the market along with knowledgeable sales people who can solve most organizing problems. Almost one-third of the store is filled with home office furniture that ranges from basic to more sophisticated. Their U-shaped and L-shaped units can be configured to fit most home offices.

Fellowes Manufacturing Company
www.fellowes.com

Home office workers everywhere continue to rely on Fellowes' line of ergonomically correct accessories, shredders, desk organizers and other products.

The Mobile Office Outfitter
www.mobilegear.com

Check out this site for mobile accessories, including car organizers, mobile desks and laptop accessories.

The Museum of Useful Things
www.themut.com

Do you need an unusual pen and pencil holder? Do you like items with a retro feel, or hard-to-find office accessories? If so, you'll enjoy visiting this site. Many products are made of aluminum or steel and are, as the site suggests, useful.

Office Depot

www.officedepot.com

During your visits to the office supply store for supplies, equipment or desk accessories, you've probably noticed an entire section of the store dedicated to furniture. Most of the furniture available at these office supply superstores is Ready-to-Assemble (RTA). (For a small fee, you can hire someone to assemble your new furniture at your home office.) Sales associates are generally knowledgeable about the furniture, but if not, you'll find plenty of literature on each desk to answer most questions.

Office Max

www.officemax.com

This office supply superstore offers everything from staplers to printers to furniture at competitive prices.

OttLite

www.ottlite.com

Eyestrain and fatigue often can be attributed to poor lighting. If you want to reduce glare and diminish distortion, try the OttLite ®. Its ability to closely replicate natural daylight along with its beautiful design makes this the ideal choice for any home office.

See Jane Work

www.seejanework.com

If you're looking for stylish, functional and out-of-the-ordinary office supplies and accessories, you'll enjoy this site. You'll find colorful, fun, and useful products that are more interesting than the products you'll find at an office supply superstore. They carry calendars, files, bulletin boards and interesting gifts for the hard-to-please home office professional.

Solutions

www.solutionscatalog.com

This site bills its line as "products that make life easier" and this online company really is a good source of products for inside and outside your home.

Stacks & Stacks
www.stacksandstacks.com
> Whether you need organizing products for your home or home office, Stacks & Stacks offers thousands of stylish products.

Staples
www.staples.com
> This office supply superstore offers many of the same products as others superstores with comparable prices. You can purchase items online, via their catalog or at one of their hundreds of stores.

West Elm
www.westelm.com
> West Elm offers contemporary home office furniture and desk accessories. Their furniture is simple yet stylish.

ABOUT LISA KANAREK

Lisa Kanarek is one of the nation's leading home office experts and the author of several books, including *Home Office Solutions, Organizing Your Home Business* and *101 Home Office Success Secrets.* As one of only a handful of home office experts who is also an interior designer, Lisa brings to every project her extensive home office knowledge and design expertise. She advises corporations and individuals on all aspects of working from home and writes the blog, Working Naked (www.workingnaked.com).

Lisa has been a guest on several national programs including *Good Morning America, CNN Financial News, CBS Up-to-the-Minute, CNBC, American Public Radio, Movie & a Makeover,* and *Public Radio's Marketplace.* Lisa has been featured — as an author and in interviews — in hundreds of publications including *The Wall Street Journal, The New York Times, Newsweek, Success, Money, Entrepreneur, Cosmopolitan, Dwell, Kiplinger's Personal Finance* and *Redbook.*